D1643833

Lighthouse Products

The image of the lighthouse has long caught the imagination and has been reproduced as a vast range of manufactured goods. The centenary of John Smeaton's Eddystone Lighthouse off Plymouth, where a lighthouse in various forms has stood since 1698, was deemed so significant that the Royal Mint commissioned its image to appear on new coinage issued in 1860. A later image of the lighthouse was used on the penny from 1937 until its decimalisation in 1971.

Lighthouses have also been a popular theme for souvenir collectors since seaside day-trips surged in popularity during the nineteenth century. Holidaymakers could carry home tokens like thimbles, biscuit tins and the china models produced in vast quantities by the Staffordshire potters, Goss China. For years, visitors to Alum Bay on the Isle of Wight copied their Victorian forebears by taking away a glass model of a lighthouse, filled with the coloured sand for which the bay is famous.

The lighthouse is celebrated by the British Year of the Sea in 2005, with a range of products available from National Trust shops. Several Trust properties, including South Foreland Lighthouse, the White Cliffs of Dover and Souter Lighthouse, sell gift items that include bookmarks, cross-stitch kits

and photograph frames. And further afield, lighthouse collectibles are available from lighthouses, museums and specialist websites, both in the UK and abroad.

left: Lighthouse Brand salmon label, c.1910-20

above: Searchlight Matches, c.1920

right: Lighthouse tin for Lyons Assorted Toffees, incorporating a calendar, c.1920

National Trust Enterprises
Orderline tel: 0870 112 5384
Web: www.nationaltrust-shop.co.uk

South Foreland Lighthouse
St Margaret's Bay, Dover,
Kent CT15 6HP
Tel: 01304 852463
Email: southforeland@nationaltrust.org.uk

The White Cliffs of Dover
Gateway Visitor Centre,
Langdon Cliffs, Dover, Kent CT16 1HJ
Tel: 01304 202756
Email: whitecliffs@nationaltrust.org.uk

Souter Lighthouse
Coast Road, Whitburn, Sunderland,
Tyne and Wear SR6 7NH
Tel: 0191 529 3161
Email: souter@nationaltrust.org.uk

For museums and lighthouses,
both abroad and in the UK, see
*Lighthouse Accommodation: Britain
and Worldwide* by Joy Adcock (2003).
ISBN 0 9535182 1 3

For lighthouse-themed music, visit
www.beachcombermusic.com

See also www.nauticalia.com for a
wide range of marine and lighthouse
products.

*The information above is accurate at
the time of going to press.*

Staying in a Lighthouse

Dozens of lighthouses and their surrounding properties are available to rent for holidays, allowing visitors to get a taste of what life was like for lighthouse keepers. The National Trust owns several holiday properties attached to or close to lighthouses, including:

The Keeper's and Engineer's Cottages at Souter on the Northumberland coast, the first lighthouse in the world to be lit by electricity and one-time home of Grace Darling's nephew Robert.

Lynmouth Lighthouse Keepers' Cottage at Foreland Point on the north Devon coast, built in 1900 on the cliffs overlooking the Bristol Channel.

The Coastguard Cottages, situated above the nineteenth-century Needles Old Battery on the Isle of Wight, where visitors can see foghorns from the original lighthouse and the submarine cable which powers today's automatic lighthouse.

The Coastguard Cottages at Peppercombe, near Clovelly in north Devon. These cottages can be rented from the National Trust for holidays

For details of these and other properties, contact:
The National Trust Holiday Booking Office,
PO Box 536, Melksham,
Wiltshire SN12 8SX
Tel: 0870 4584422
Fax: 0870 4584400
Email: cottages@nationaltrust.org.uk
or visit our website:
www.nationaltrustcottages.co.uk

Trinity House Lighthouse Service, in association with Rural Retreats, also rents out lighthouse keepers' cottages on sites in England, Wales and the Channel Islands. For information, contact:
Rural Retreats,
Draycott Business Centre,
Draycott, Moreton-in-Marsh,
Gloucestershire GL56 9JY
Tel: 01386 701177
Email: info@ruralretreats.co.uk
Web: www.ruralretreats.co.uk

More adventurous holiday-makers can join *THV Patricia*, the flagship of the Trinity House Fleet, as her crew carry out their vital work of maintaining lighthouses and lightships. For more information, contact Trinity House on:
Tel: 01255 245034
Email: contractual.services@thls.org
Web: www.trinityhouse.biz

For other contacts in the UK and abroad, see:

The National Trust for Scotland
Holidays Department
Tel: 0131 243 9331
Email: holidays@nts.org.uk
Web: www.nts.org.uk

The Landmark Trust
Shottesbrooke, Maidenhead,
Berkshire SL6 3S
Tel: 01628 825925
Email: bookings@landmarktrust.org.uk
Web: www.landmarktrust.org.uk

Joy Adcock, of the Association of Lighthouse Keepers, published *Lighthouse Accommodation: Britain and Worldwide* in 2003. This useful guide gives contacts and booking details for accommodation, as well as information on visitor centres and museums in the UK and abroad.
ISBN 0 9535182 1 3

Maritime Heritage

You can use the contacts below as a starting point to explore Britain's outstanding maritime life and history.

For a comprehensive online guide to maritime museums, sites and facilities in the UK, visit the Maritime Britain site:
www.maritimebritain.fsnet.co.uk

The Association of Lighthouse Keepers,
Mike Millichamp, Membership Secretary, 9 Gwel Trencrom, Hayle, Cornwall TR27 6PJ
Web: www.lighthouse.fsnet.co.uk

'Leading Lights' – The International Lighthouse Journal,
Milford Marina, Milford Haven, Pembrokeshire SA73 3AF
Tel: 01646 698825
Fax: 01646 692896
Email: peter.williams@leadinglights.net
Web: www.leadinglights.net

The Lighthouse Society of Great Britain, Gravesend Cottage, Torpoint, Cornwall PL11 2LX
Email: ktrethewey@btinternet.com

World Lighthouse Society,
The Lantern House, 63 Bacton Road, North Walsham, Norfolk NR28 9DS
Tel: 01692 403784
Email: rosalie@davisgibb.fslife.co.uk
Web: www.worldlighthouses.org

The Northern Lighthouse Board (for lighthouses in Scotland and the Isle of Man),
84 George Street,
Edinburgh EH2 3DA
Tel: 0131 473 3100
Fax: 0131 220 2093
Email: enquiries@nlb.org.uk
Web: www.nlb.org.uk

The Commissioners of Irish Lights (for lighthouses throughout Ireland),
16 Lower Pembroke Street,
Dublin 2, Eire
Tel: (00) 353 1 632 1900
Email: info@cil.ie
Web: www.cil.ie

Maritime Heritage Tours,
Michael Walter, Corston House,
56 Spencer Road, Ryde,
Isle of Wight PO33 3AD
Email: m_walters@martours.demon.co.uk

The National Trust owns many sites of interest for lighthouse enthusiasts, including:

The Lizard Wireless Station at Bass Point in south Cornwall, the site of Marconi's historic wireless experiments in 1901.
Tel: 01326 290384
Web: www.lizardwireless.org

The Marconi Centre at Poldhu in south Cornwall, which houses an exhibition funded by the Marconi Company.
Tel: 01326 241656
Web: www.mulliononline.com

Orford Ness National Nature Reserve in Suffolk, a secret military test site from 1913 until the mid-1980s, and home to the most powerful light on the east coast of England.
Tel: 01394 450057
Email: orfordness@nationaltrust.org.uk

South Foreland Lighthouse on the White Cliffs of Dover in Kent, where Michael Faraday experimented with the use of electricity in lighthouses.
Tel: 01304 852463
Email: southforeland@nationaltrust.org.uk

Souter Lighthouse on the north-east coast in Tyne and Wear, the first lighthouse to be lit by electricity
Tel: 01670 773966
Email: souter@nationaltrust.org.uk

The Gribbin Daymark near Fowey in south Cornwall, an 84-foot high tower that visitors can climb on summer Sundays. For opening times, tel: 01208 265235 or 01726 870146.

The information above, which does not represent a comprehensive listing, is accurate at the time of going to press.

Selected Bibliography

Adcock, Joy
Lighthouse Accommodation: Britain and Worldwide (2003)

Armstrong, Richard
Grace Darling – Maid and Myth (1965)

Bathurst, Bella
The lighthouse Stevensons: the extraordinary story of the building of the Scottish lighthouses by the ancestors of Robert Louis Stevenson (1999)

Hague, Douglas
Lighthouses of Wales: Their Architecture and Archaeology (1994)

Hague, Douglas and Christie, Rosemary
Lighthouses: Their Architecture, History and Archaeology (1975)

Hart-Davis, Adam
Henry Winstanley and the Eddystone Lighthouse (2002)

Naish, John
Seamarks: Their History and Development (1985)

Nicholson, Christopher
Rock Lighthouses of Britain (1983)

Williams, Peter
Beacon on the Rock: the dramatic history of lighthouses from Ancient Greece to the present day (c.2001)

Woodman, Richard & Wilson, Jane
The Lighthouses of Trinity House (2002)

Picture Credits

Index

First published in Great Britain in
2005 by National Trust Enterprises
Limited, 36 Queen Anne's Gate,
London SW1H 9AS
www.nationaltrust.org.uk
Registered charity number 205846

ISBN 0 7078 0397 7

Designed by TRUE
Printed and bound in Hong Kong

Front cover: Souter Lighthouse,
Tyne and Wear, photographed in 1992
(NTPL/Matthew Antrobus)

Back cover: Beachy Head Lighthouse,
East Sussex (NTPL/David Sellman)